LIFE BEYOND
CONFUSION AND FEAR

# LIFE BEYOND
# CONFUSION AND FEAR

▼

*Cathryn L Taylor*

iUniverse, Inc.
New York  Lincoln  Shanghai

LIFE BEYOND CONFUSION AND FEAR

Copyright © 2005 by CATHRYN TAYLOR

iUniverse books may be ordered through booksellers or by contacting:

iUniverse
2021 Pine Lake Road, Suite 100
Lincoln, NE 68512
www.iuniverse.com
1-800-Authors (1-800-288-4677)

ISBN-13: 978-0-595-36474-9 (pbk)
ISBN-13: 978-0-595-80906-6 (ebk)
ISBN-10: 0-595-36474-8 (pbk)
ISBN-10: 0-595-80906-5 (ebk)

Printed in the United States of America

As I prepare this manuscript for publication it occurs to me that represented in these pages are twenty-five years of my life's work. I have lived what I have taught and am proud of how I have used the experiences my Soul charted.

I did not do it alone. There are many, too many to name, who took my hand; had my back; caught my tears and encouraged me to grow.

Yet, I cannot send this work out into the world without acknowledging the circle of women who, over the years, have held me strong to my integrity, comforted my inner children, celebrated my joy and loved me beyond my confusion and fear.

**This book is dedicated to**

Margee Bartle  Marsha Norris  Darlene Turner
Donna Fox  Laurel King
Alyssa Hall  Tama Adelmen
Marie Kaley  Ana Maria
Nancy  Dean  Jennifer Traber

# Contents

# PREFACE

*We are a society in mourning with few adult tools to grieve. The recent events of terrorism and war coupled with current stresses of daily life leave us afraid and confused—triggering childhood wounds and adult doubts about our ability to cope. It is common to express this unresolved confusion, fear, grief and tension through compulsive and addictive behaviors.*

*We may eat too much; drink, drug or smoke too much; love, shop, work, gamble or worry too much. We slowly begin to live out of fear rather than faith—compulsion rather than choice—isolation rather than unity as we long to anchor our safety in a place that cannot be bombed, high-jacked or murdered.*

**How Vulnerable Are YOU to DAILY STRESS?**
Do you give and receive affection regularly?
Do you get strength from your spiritual/religious beliefs?
Are you able to speak openly about your feelings?
Do you do something for fun at least one time a week?
Are you able to organize your time effectively?
Do you take quiet time for yourself daily?
**2 or more No's and you are experiencing daily stress!**

**How Vulnerable Were YOU to CHILDHOOD STRESS?**
Did you feel revered and respected as a child?
Were you able to speak your truth in your family?
Was your family close to relatives or friends?
Were your parents friendly with each other?
Did you have childhood friends who you trusted?
Do you remember feeling safe as a child?
**2 or more No's and you are suffering from childhood stress!**

**How Vulnerable Are YOU to Global Stress?**
Do you still feel fear with respect to the events of 9/11?
Do you feel an impending sense of doom?
Are you afraid to fly or feel a fear of crowds?
Are you afraid to open your mail or do you avoid the news?
Do you fear someone you love will have to go to war?
Do you feel more frightened about daily events than before 9/11?
**2 or more Yes's and you are experiencing Global stress!**

The stress we feel in our lives, if not resolved, gets expressed through maladaptive methods of coping which ultimately reveal themselves in physical ailments or injuries, psychological unrest, spiritual isolation or compulsive and addictive behaviors.

This model offers a way out.

# From tragedies To triumphs

For some it began as early as Pearl Harbor or the Korean War. For the baby boomers it was the assassinations and unrest of the '60's, the Watergate scandal, and the Viet Nam War. '*Eye Witness Minute to Minute News*' exacerbated the phenomenon. It brought the reality of unpredictability into the middle of our own homes as many witnessed, 'live and in living color' the tragedy of the space shuttle, Challenger, and deaths from John Kennedy and Princess Diana.

When these global events mix with the unpredictable eruptions of mother nature—such as the destruction of hurricanes in the East, the earthquakes and fires on the California coast and tornadoes and river floods of the Midwest—which then co-mingle with the stress most of us experience in our daily pursuits, we end up feeling overwhelmed, afraid—out of control and full of despair. Nothing eroded the general sense of safety and trust more than the tragedies of 9/11. That event affected the world as a whole and few lives will ever again be the same.

How do we cope? How do we deal with this mass grief as it weaves with our personal grief? We don't. Although the fires dwindle at ground zero, in most of the hearts of America, they rage within. We are a society in mourning with few adult tools to grieve. These recent events, coupled with the stresses of day-to-day life, have thrown most of us into the aftermath of confusion and fear—struggling with an underlying anxiety that erupts in our living rooms, in the workplace, on the freeways and in every area of our lives. We want to emulate the sense of solidarity we viewed on our televisions and saw in the streets of our nation, but most of us are confused how to create that unity within.

Yet, tragedies—personal and global alike—*can* ignite a determination in us to break out of our shell and move beyond our immediate response of confusion and fear.

## *Exercise 1:*

*Think for a moment about what existed before the 9/11 tragedy. For most it was complacency and denial. What was the quality of your life before the incidents of 9/11—and how is it now different?*

_____

_____

_____

_____

_____

_____

_____

_____

_____

_____

_____

_____

_____

_____

_____

_____

_____

_____

_____

_____

_____

_____

_____

_____

_____

_____

_____

_____

## DISCUSSION:

Before 9/11 most of us were caught up in our day-to-day life of routine and predictability? It is common to go through our daily lives unaware of our thoughts and feelings—to take on an almost robotic frame of mind. Tragedies knock us out of that robotic state and plummet us into a state of confusion and fear.

Whether personal or global, they offer us an opportunity to identify our complacency and rise to the expression of parts of ourselves which usually lie dormant.

### Exercise 2:

*Reflect for a moment on your own life. What personal events have occurred that shook you out of your own complacency? How did you respond? Were you able to move beyond feeling victimized? Were you able rise to the occasion and discover an inner strength that was not accessible to you in your day-to-day life? If not, can you now, in hindsight, see glimpses of that strength?*

_____
_____
_____
_____
_____
_____
_____
_____
_____
_____
_____
_____
_____
_____
_____
_____
_____
_____
_____
_____
_____

## DISCUSSION:

When we suffer an isolated tragedy that impacts only us—such as a divorce or a crippling accident—there can be an isolation in our fear and confusion. Yet, it can, nonetheless, force us into aspects of our being which we would not have accessed before the tragedy. In spite of our isolation and fear we often find a renewed sense of our connection to God. When a group suffers a tragedy—whether it is a family, nation or world—there is another element which takes place and that is the renowned sense of community that results from shared grief.

One of the functions of funerals, for those who are left behind, is that every one who attends had a relationship with the person who passed on. Each person has his or her unique point of reference for the loss. That point of reference and commonality creates a bridge of closeness which defies the isolation of loss.

The same can be said for tragedies which occur on a global level. What was profound about the events of 9/11 was the global impact it had on each of us. That shared experience dissolved a sense of isolation as we each shared in our respective loss. The gift of 9/11 was that it knocked us out of our complacency collectively. It became our new, *shared* point of reference for we each had our "story" to tell as to where we were, what we were doing, how we felt and what we did. The personal and public loss was the same and, for a while, there was no isolation in our grief. The tragedy opened our hearts and legitimized an examination of our grief because no one escaped response.

This model and the accompanying classes and consultations invite you to take that process one step further. You will be inspired to identify your own 9/11 incidents. For each response we had to the events of 9/11 hold within them clues as to the ways we cope with our personal tragedies. Through this model you will be invited to systematically identify the stresses in your own life and examine your effective and non-effective methods of coping.

Ideally, when stress occurs, we know how to deal with it effectively. We talk about it and release the tension through appropriate physical activity. We know how to make the feelings manageable so we can resolve the the pain and move on. But few of us know how to do this. Typically, we act out instead; we do whatever we need to do to get away from the discomfort of the tension. We grab a cigarette, stuff our mouths with food, obsess about someone else, or numb out to TV or with drugs or booze. Our society values little else. Every commercial we watch, every billboard we see, every magazine advertisement we glance at gives us ways to escape feeling—not methods with which we can deal with feelings.

So what do we do? We do anything that will relieve the stress. Some of us eat too much, others drink too much, some smoke too much, and others love, shop, work or worry too much.

Whatever we do, we do it to excess. In our struggle to relieve the anxiety of our tension, we end up actually increasing it. We lack the skills needed to know what to do differently. We have not learned how to live with feelings; we have only learned how to escape them.

*End of Introduction*

# CHAPTER ONE:

## CYCLE ONE:

▼

# THE ORIGINS OF CONFUSION AND FEAR

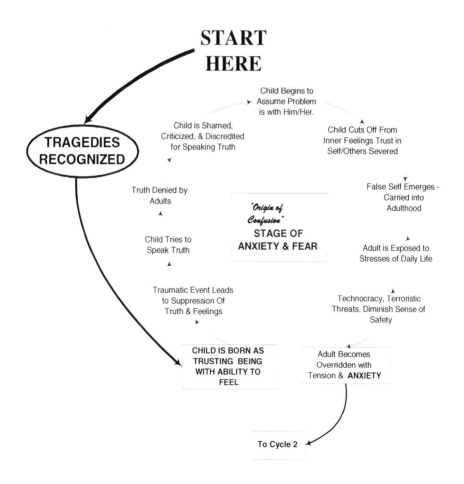

**START HERE**

Child Begins to Assume Problem is with Him/Her.

Child is Shamed, Criticized, & Discredited for Speaking Truth

Child Cuts Off From Inner Feelings Trust in Self/Others Severed

**TRAGEDIES RECOGNIZED**

Truth Denied by Adults

*"Origin of Confusion"* **STAGE OF ANXIETY & FEAR**

False Self Emerges - Carried into Adulthood

Child Tries to Speak Truth

Adult is Exposed to Stresses of Daily Life

Traumatic Event Leads to Suppression Of Truth & Feelings

Technocracy, Terroristic Threats, Diminish Sense of Safety

**CHILD IS BORN AS TRUSTING BEING WITH ABILITY TO FEEL**

Adult Becomes Overridden with Tension & **ANXIETY**

To Cycle 2

When we were children we knew how to live with feelings. In fact, that's all we did. If you have ever been around an infant, it is obvious they are "living with feeling!" When they hurt, they cry. When they are hungry, they let you know. When they are tired of being held, they squirm until they are put down. Our natural state of existence is to be very connected to what we feel. The connection to our feelings we have as children is often not nurtured. Instead, it is squelched. It is squelched through the spoken and unspoken rules that each family unknowingly adopts.

Most families respond to their internal and the external stress by unconsciously adopting a set of spoken or unspoken rules. In It Will Never Happen to Me (Medical Administration, Colorado, 1980), Claudia Black identified the most classic rules in a dysfunctional family:

## DON'T TALK

It is not safe to speak the truth about the family stress. It is either denied or the truthsayer is humiliated and shamed.

## DON'T TRUST

One learns he or she cannot trust what is seen, felt or heard…promises are broken, incidents are twisted to sustain the denial and feelings are dismissed.

## DON'T FEEL

Family members learn that it does not benefit them to be in touch with feelings—there is no comfort for the pain and no acknowledgement for the emotion or perception of reality.

## *Exercise 3:*

*Take a moment to reflect on what the rules in your own family were. What were you not allowed to discuss? What could you not trust and what was unsafe to feel? Record your responses below.*

_____

_____

_____

_____

_____

_____

_____

_____

_____

_____

_____

_____

_____

_____

_____

_____

_____

_____

_____

_____

_____

_____

_____

_____

_____

_____

_____

_____

_____

_____

_____

## DISCUSSION:

Until the generation of baby-boomer parents, feelings were not valued. Instead children were molded and trained at home, school and church to discount what they felt. The result was that individuals learned to devalue feelings. They learned to ignore their inner knowingness. They learned that speaking their truth was unacceptable. And if they did not learn it quickly, they were shamed, discredited or teased into learning it. This socialization was passed from generation to generation as individuals learned to disconnect from their "real self" in order to become acceptable members of their families and communities. Most of us grew up with the expectation that we had to be like everyone else so we developed behaviors like everyone else. The more socialized we became, the more disconnected from our true selves we were.

But socialization did work. For many generations, this disconnection from who we really were so we could fit in to our families and our communities worked, because it was here that our sense of security was to be found. Our environment was stable and intact. It was common to know our neighbors and to live in the same community for our whole life. This kind of permanence provided security and stability. We needed that in order to survive.

So traditional parenting and teaching methods and the religious practices we experienced in church were all effective tools of the socialization process because they helped us develop socially acceptable behaviors. Even though it required disconnecting from our real self and developing a false one, it was functional.

It no longer is. It hasn't been for quite some time. World War II marked the end of permanence in our society. As the economy and technology improved, we became more mobile. We left families and communities and stability behind. As we moved into the decade of the Sixties, we left our idealism behind. Assassinations, the struggle for Civil Rights, and a senseless war left us wounded and apathetic. The Seventies brought Watergate, a focus on the Nuclear Arms Race and disillusionment. In the Eighties we found ourselves in limbo…the Nineties brought more isolation and disillusionment. We were disconnected from others, but not yet reconnected to our real self or feelings. Now, more than ever before, this connection is essential.

In today's world, a connection to our intuition or real self and an ability to know and process feelings are absolutely essential. But we still lack the skills. The Post-War "Baby Boomer" generation was the first generation to be raised to become a part of a society where these skills were necessary. Each generation since has felt more and more displaced and unprepared for modern day challenges. The incidents of 9/11 simply made this fact more pronounced.

This displacement from family and community creates anxiety. A lack of connection to our real self creates anxiety. The over-stimulation of choices and expectations presented to us by a complex, unstable and potentially violent society creates anxiety. Anxiety is unpleasant—so we seek to escape it.

*End of Chapter One*

# CHAPTER TWO:

▼

# THE CYCLES OF COMPULSIONS AND ADDICTIONS

Excessive acting out *(maladaptive expression of feelings)* helps us succeed, temporarily. It relieves the tension felt from our anxiety and it dissipates unmanageable stress. However, it also maintains and exacerbates our disconnection from our real self and intuition, which is the origin of the stress. As long as acting out helps us cope and makes stress manageable, it is constructive. The problem is knowing when it becomes excessive and destructive; the challenge is to determine when compulsions become addictions.

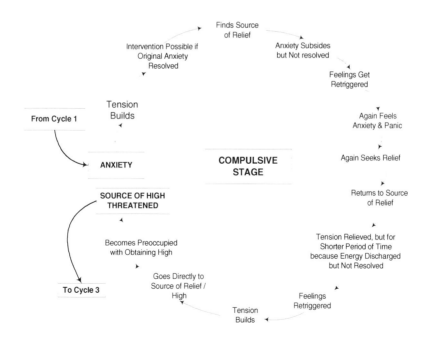

**and**

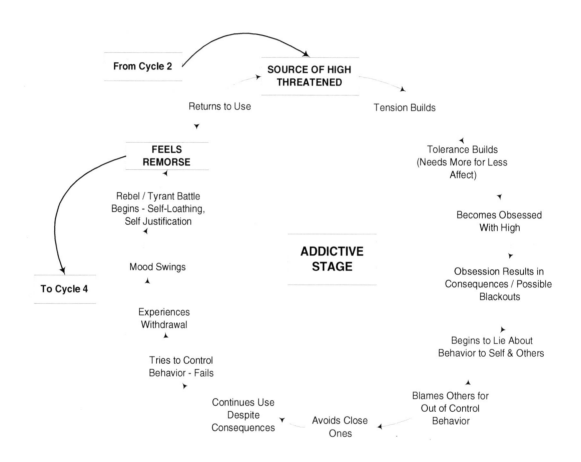

From Cycle 2

SOURCE OF HIGH
THREATENED

Returns to Use

Tension Builds

FEELS
REMORSE

Tolerance Builds
(Needs More for Less
Affect)

Rebel / Tyrant Battle
Begins - Self-Loathing,
Self Justification

Becomes Obsessed
With High

ADDICTIVE
STAGE

Mood Swings

Obsession Results in
Consequences / Possible
Blackouts

To Cycle 4

Experiences
Withdrawal

Begins to Lie About
Behavior to Self & Others

Tries to Control
Behavior - Fails

Blames Others for
Out of Control
Behavior

Continues Use
Despite
Consequences

Avoids Close
Ones

## Exercise 4:

*Think of a recent time when you were tense. How did you spell relief? What was your first response to that stress? Did it relieve the stress? Were there any residual consequences?*

_____

_____

_____

_____

_____

_____

_____

_____

_____

_____

_____

_____

_____

_____

_____

_____

_____

_____

_____

_____

_____

_____

_____

_____

_____

_____

_____

_____

_____

_____

_____

_____

_____

_____

_____

*DISCUSSION:*

When does social drinking become addictive drinking? When does a simple shopping trip become a compulsive one? How does eating one piece of cake lead to eating a whole cake then involuntary regurgitation? The answers to these questions vary. Addiction to substances such as alcohol, drugs, nicotine or some foods includes a physiological component which needs to be considered and addressed. But Ernie Larson was probably right. In his book, Second Stage Recovery, (Harper and Row, 1985) he suggests that…"when acting out becomes a habituated response to stress we have moved from a habit to a compulsion or an addiction…"

When we are addicted, we suffer consequences. In fact, the most relevant question in identifying addictions is determining whether our behavior has negative consequences. Answering this question demands honesty. Since denial is a primary characteristic of addiction, honesty is hard to find—and most of us won't find it until it hits us in the face. Most of us will not change our behavior until our actions *threaten the loss of someone or something we are not prepared to live without.* Only when our consequences become grave enough, when the tension our addictive behavior creates becomes greater than the tension it relieves, do we hit bottom. If we are lucky, when we hit bottom, we find ourselves in recovery and/or therapy.

# Use the chart on the following page to determine the degree to which your compulsions and addictions have progressed.

# PERSONALIZED PROGRESSION CHART

*How has your excessive behavior progressed? Please place an X on the line before each symptom you have experienced.*

## EARLY STAGE OF COMPULSIVE BEHAVIORS

_____Sneaks around so others do not see you engaging in habit
_____Becomes preoccupied with habit (i.e. eating smoking, drinking)
_____Avoids reference to the uncomfortable behavior
_____Tolerance increases with respect to quantity and frequency
_____Behaves compulsively to seek relief—to relieve tension
_____Feels uncomfortable in social situations—so uses
_____Experiences loss of control
_____Becomes dishonest about habit
_____Frequency of compulsive behaviors increases

## TRANSITION FROM COMPULSIVE TO ADDICTIVE STAGE

_____Hides evidence of habit (stashes food, hides bills, bottles etc)
_____Experiences panic when triggered to act out but unable to do so
_____Tries to control behavior (stops-starts and stops–starts again)
_____Hears disapproving comments from others regarding habit
_____Begins to rationalize behavior
_____Feels grandiose when drunk, high or running addictive energy
_____Feels guilt about habit
_____Neglects other activities or responsibilities
_____Resentments begin to build towards others for intervening
_____Devalues personal relationships

## CHRONIC STAGE OF ADDICTIONS

_____Considers geographic escape (moving, changing jobs, etc)
_____Sexual drive decreases
_____Quits or loses job because habit interferes
_____Again tries to control habit, but fails
_____Feels continuous remorse
_____Becomes totally preoccupied with habit
_____Has identifiable fears associated with addiction
_____Unable to work or concentrate on other tasks
_____Deterioration of moral standards begins
_____Loses important relationships, family/friends
_____Exhausts all alibis
_____HITS BOTTOM (threat of losing something unprepared to live without)

With this assessment fresh, let's now look at the tasks of each of the three stages of recovery and how the inner child/ren emerge in each stage.

# Tasks and needs of the inner children as they emerge in the three stages of recovery

STAGE ONE OF RECOVERY
TASK: To intervene in addictive behavior and to learn how to cope with daily activities without relapsing.
INNER CHILDREN: Are blurred and non-specific.
OVERALL NEED: To bond and feel safe in recovery.

STAGE TWO OF RECOVERY
TASK: To confront the underlying reasons that lead to compulsive and addictive behavior and to repair and resolve the past.
INNER CHILDREN: Begin to emerge as different ages with specific issues that need to be addressed.
OVERALL NEED: To solidify the adult self who can interact with the different ages within and begin to heal the past.

STAGE THREE OF RECOVERY
TASK: To reclaim the "God Within."
INNER CHILDREN: Become integrated and are the foundation for the creative self.
OVERALL NEED: To free one's creativity by accessing the qualities of the Higher Self, the Adult Self, and the Child Selves.

# Developmental Needs at Each Stage of Recovery

*Tasks that need to be mastered at each stage of development and how they manifest in adult life if this does not occur.*

*How needs are met in:*

| | Stage 1 | Stage 2 | Stage 3 |
|---|---|---|---|
| **Birth to 18 months:** Task is to bond and to feel safe. In adulthood experienced as fear of abandonment, difficulty with bonding and a perpetual feeling of being unsafe. | Bonds with group. Consistency/ Structure of meetings provide sense of safety. | Bonds with adult self or internalized parental figure. | Bonds and becomes symbiotic with Higher Power. |
| **18 months to 3 yrs:** Task is to begin to separate and to learn about boundaries and setting limits. Seen in adulthood as loose or rigid boundaries, becomes a clinger or a distancer, can have difficulty saying no because of fear of rejection. | Separates from addictive behavior with the support of the group. | Adult self separates from pain of inner children and helps younger selves individuate. | Existential separateness tolerated because of relation to Higher Power. |
| **3 yrs to 6 yrs old:** Task is to learn how to accept and negotiate between good and bad parts of self. Learns about shame and guilt. Failure to accomplish this is seen in adulthood as all or nothing thinking, criticalness of self and others, self-loathing and negative inner dialogue. | 4th step separates guilt from shame, no crosstalk allows for acceptance; sharing provides model. | Adult self helps inner children accept each other and all feelings. | 6th & 7th steps help remove defects; compassion received from Higher Power. |
| **6 yrs to 13 yrs old:** Task is to learn how to fit in with peers, how to start and finish projects, and to identify with adult figures outside of home. Difficulty manifests in adulthood as inability to begin and finish projects, insecurity with fitting in, and need for relationships with people older than self. | Program accepts each person where he or she is at. Working steps with sponsor gives experiences of completion/ fitting in. | Inner adult and sponsor help inner children with isolation/ exclusion, and projects. | Connection to Higher Power provides a sense of belonging to something bigger than self. |
| **Adolescence:** Task is to deal with social and sexual awkwardness, to carve out a sense of self, to again separate and become independent. | Intimacy with many reduces awkwardness, autonomizes by working steps. | Adult self helps inner teen through stages of growing up. | Connection to Higher Power helps the development of belief in higher plan and purpose. |

*End Of Chapter Two*

# CHAPTER THREE:
# RECOVERY STAGE ONE:

# "SEEKING HELP—INTERVENING IN MALADAPTIVE BEHAVIOR"

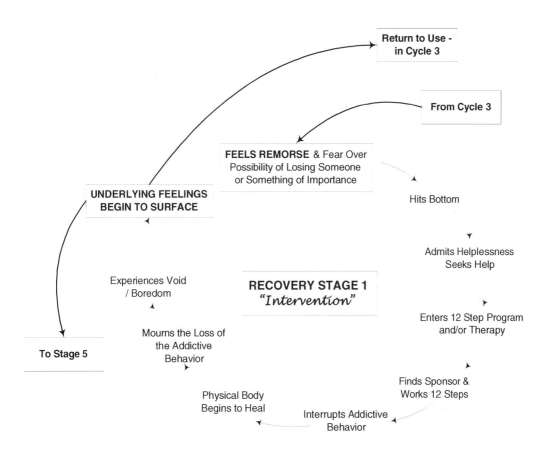

Once we allow ourselves to seek help, we begin to re-experience some level of feeling. In fact, we are usually raw with many mixed feelings. This emotional confusion is the culmination of the disowned feelings from childhood. Void of the numbing effect of our addictions and maladaptive behaviors we are quickly thrown back to the coping mechanisms of childhood.

When we experience a sudden rush of anxiety, it is really our inner child's grief. When we sit in self-help or therapy meetings rehearsing what we want to say, it is really our inner child seeking approval. When we fear rejection or exposure, it is really our inner child's shame. When we re-experience our compulsion to act out or use, it is our attempt to numb the inner child's pain. When we sit in meetings and fantasize about that piece of chocolate cake or that cigarette or drink, it is our inner child's ambivalence. Those moments we want to act out the most are the times we are closest to the repressed feelings of our inner child. Until we learn how to deal with and heal the pain of our past, we are forever vulnerable to returning to our old addictive ways. The ways in which we do this vary according to the specific needs, which emerge in each stage of recovery. Initially, however, it is important to understand that until we allow our inner child to feel and release what was unsafe to experience in childhood and until we reclaim the natural, creative energy which exists within, we are at risk.

What exactly is the inner child?

Dealing with the inner child is not a new concept to recovery. In fact, according to Charles Whitfield, author of Healing the Child Within, (Health Communications, Inc., 1986) "the concept has been around for over two thousand years. Carl Jung called it the "divine child," Emmet Fox called it the "wonder child." Psychotherapists Alice Miller and Donald Winnicott refer to it as the "true self." Dorothy Corkille-Briggs (Celebrate Yourself, Doubleday, 1977) and Eric Berne, founder of Transactional Analysis were among the first to discuss the "wounded" or "not ok" child. They began addressing the issues related to the part of us who is damaged in childhood and feels ashamed and afraid. Nathaniel Braden was one of the first to link low self-esteem to the traumas experienced in childhood. In his books, How to Raise Your Self-Esteem (Bantam 1987) and Experience High Self-Esteem (Simon & Schuster, 1988) he offered concrete ways of raising one's self-esteem through exercises which reclaimed, healed and integrated the unresolved feelings from childhood.

Claudia Black and Sharon Wegsheider-Cruse were among the first to introduce the concept of the dysfunctional family to the field of chemical dependency. In It Will Never Happen to Me (Medical Administration, Colorado, 1980), Claudia identified particular characteristics that were common in children raised in alcoholic homes. She coined the phrase "Adult Children of Alcoholics" because, in her own recovery and in her work with others, she began to notice that many adults from alcoholic homes carried certain childhood patterns into their adult lives. Sharon

Wegsheider-Curse, in <u>Another Chance</u> (Science and Behavior Books, Inc., 1981) added even more insight into the family dynamics found in alcoholic homes.

Perhaps no one connected the concepts of the inner child, the dysfunctional family and addictions together more than John Bradshaw. With his series and book on the family and his subsequent book, <u>Healing the Shame That Binds Us</u> (Health Communications, Inc., 1988) the field of addiction experienced an explosion. For many, the pieces began to make sense and the world or recovery boomed. Twelve Step meetings popped up everywhere and for every subject. They became the new "bar" of the eighties. Even though the term "Inner Child" got thrown around quite freely there was still much confusion. Once people found their inner child, they did not know how to work with the childhood pain, and they were unclear as to what stage of recovery they should begin.

We begin to heal the inner child the moment we seek help. It starts by simply participating in any kind of meeting where we hear others voice the same or similar feelings as our own. Slowly we begin to experience an acceptance and a bonding between others and us takes place. As this occurs we begin to feel connected to something bigger than our addictions or our pain. The raw emotions of the inner child start feeling more manageable. We begin to learn how to successfully cope with the feelings of our day-to-day life without acting out.

This is perhaps the first step in learning to effectively manage our daily lives. The initial discomfort that emerges is usually a sort of floating anxiety. With time, it dissolves. It is unlikely these initial feelings are directly connected to any childhood trauma. It seems to be unwise to focus on childhood scenes and attempt to work with the "underlying causes" of our behavior this early in our healing. If memories come, it works best to acknowledge their origin, but to remain focused on learning *how to cope with current feelings.* Uncovering buried feelings creates more anxiety. This can overwhelm a person in the early stages of healing and precipitate a return to active addiction and sabotage. It is for this reason that supportive psychotherapy aimed at helping us connect with a self-help group and developing "coping" skills is most effective. A treatment program which specializes in your specific addiction is also helpful, but your main focus should be on learning how to cope with feelings. We cannot deal with feelings if we do not know how to live with feeling non-addictively.

The first feeling we need to learn to cope with in the initial stage of healing is panic. Panic is the first stage of grief. When we stop a behavior, which we have used for a lone time, we grieve. It is a loss. The maladaptive or addictive behavior has been our best friend. As we give it up, we need support.

## Exercise 5:

Read each item carefully. Check those with which you now—or at some point in your early recovery—have experienced. Those areas to which you respond with a 'yes' can give you clues as to which inner children may be emerging in this initial stage of recovery.

*Infant Stage (Birth to 18 mos.)* Issues of Bonding, trust, intimacy, safety

_____1.  I am afraid of opening up and getting too close to others in these meetings or groups. I may get hurt.

_____2.  I have a hard time trusting this program and the people in it.

_____3.  I would like to go to other self help meetings or therapy groups but find it difficult to do so.

_____4.  I have difficulty defining my views of a Higher Source.

*Toddler Stage (18 mos-3 years.)* Issues of discernment, boundaries

_____1.  I have good intentions of working my recovery program but have a hard time following through.

_____2.  I feel ambivalent about this program—I want me/us to get help but fear what that means.

_____3.  I act like I agree with the feedback received from others when I really don't.

_____4.  I/we spend more money since getting into recovery than my/our budget permits.

*3—6 Year Old Stage* Issues of shame and guilt, discomfort in and with body

_____1.  I wish others would work the program or be as invested in the healing process as I am.

_____2.  I do not speak up in these groups and meetings for fear of what others might think.

_____3.  I find myself sitting in meetings or self-help groups being critical and judgmental of what others say and do.

_____4.  I limit what I say around others because I fear what they might think if they really knew my past.

*Grade School Self (6 to 12 years)* Issues of inclusion/exclusion, procrastination, public speaking

_____1.  I seem to always feel I am on the outside looking in.

_____2.  I stick to myself when I come to these programs and do not socialize as much as I would like.

_____3.  I dislike speaking up in groups and meetings—I spend a lot of time rehearsing what I am going to say.

_____4.  I think all of this self-help and treatment jargon is ridiculous.

*Your Inner Teen (12 to 15)* Issues of getting comfortable with discomfort, awkwardness

_____1.  I know I wanted help and intervention but I feel so uncomfortable and self-conscious in these groups.

_____2.  I have specific Spiritual beliefs, or worse yet, I don't believe in God, and that feels like heresy here.

_____3.  I have a hard time going to new groups or being in treatment groups where I know no one.

_____4.  I would rather avoid contact with some of these people than deal with the discomfort I feel at being different than them.

*Your Inner Adolescent (15 to 17)* Issues of rebellion, of carving out a sense of self

_____1.  I am afraid to speak up in these meetings for fear my ideas will be met with disapproval.

_____2.  If he/she just had not gotten caught I/we would not even have to be in this stupid group/meeting!

_____3.  I feel so restless in these meetings—I feel like "they" want me to be like everyone else.

_____4.  I fear losing a friendship or intimate relationship if I am honest with how much I used or how I really feel.

*Young Inner Adult (17 to 21) Issues* of maturation, taking knowledge into world

_____1.  This program feels a little too religious for me.

_____2.  I seem so different than these people.

_____3.  With everyone challenging my belief system, I am beginning to doubt my own beliefs.

_____4.  When I or my loved one can just be done with this treatment and get a job our family won't have a problem.

## *Exercise 6:*

*Look at the areas to which you most relate. What are the issues of that stage? What does this information tell you about your own response to this stage of recovery? Record your thoughts and feelings in the space provided below:*

_____

_____

_____

_____

_____

_____

_____

_____

_____

_____

_____

_____

_____

_____

_____

_____

_____

_____

_____

_____

_____

_____

_____

_____

_____

_____

_____

_____

_____

_____

*One of the reasons Twelve Step or self-help groups are so effective is because they provide this group support. It is comforting to be around others who either feel or have felt the same way we do. The group connection serves as the bridge from addiction to recovery. It is the thread which reconnects us, first to others and then to ourselves.*

*End Of Chapter Three*

# CHAPTER FOUR:
## RECOVERY STAGE TWO

▼

# "HEALING THE INNER CHILD/REN"

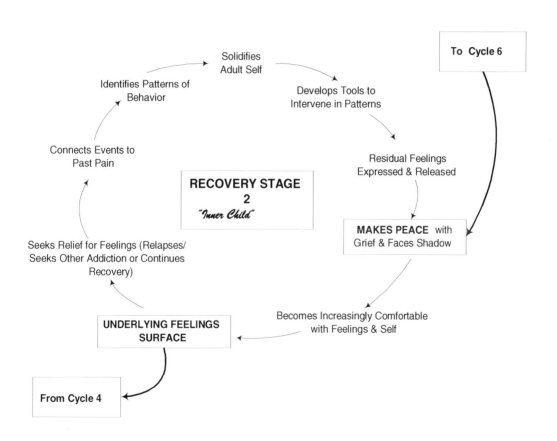

Once we feel bonded and secure within a self-help or therapy group, we move into the next stage of our healing. It is usually precipitated by the first crisis we experience without a relapse into our old coping methods. We begin the stage of loss. In this stage, we acknowledge and grieve the simple fact that our old behavior no longer works. Many of us, up until this point, have held onto the fantasy that if things got really bad, we could always go back to the old familiar way of coping—and act out addictively or self-destructively. Although this choice is always there for all of us, there comes a time when we have enough recovery and healing to know that acting out will not make us feel any better. The problem is that we do not always have the tools and knowledge to know what would alleviate our discomfort. There is a space between letting go of who we were and reclaiming who we are meant to be. This space is frightening. It is a void. It is the fourth stage of grief. It is a sense of nothingness and can be very disorienting.

This stage of healing and/or recovery can also be triggered in response to stabilizing in our growth. First we had become accustomed to the intensity of our addiction and self-sabotage; then to the preoccupation with our early recovery and healing. Oddly enough, we can miss this intensity. The intensity fed our addiction to the stress, our addiction to the adrenaline rush. It kept us away from our pain. When this intensity decreases, there is a void. It can be experienced as boredom. And boredom can feel like emotional suicide. It is disorienting and can be a time of potential relapse and a return to our old maladaptive ways if we do not take time to grieve the loss of our old ways. We have to confront the boredom and nothingness in order to get to the next level of feeling and uncover the shame and terror of the wounded self we left behind. It is through the process of reclaiming and repairing our wounded self that we rediscover our real self, our inner knowingness or intuition.

Our inner child has many ages and many scenes which need to be reworked and repaired. This process occurs in the second stage of the healing process, also referred to as the second stage of recovery.

*Abstinence from chemicals for at least twelve to twenty-four months is a must.*

"Repairenting" works with the original abandonment. It works with the underlying feelings that were repressed in our childhood. It is a process which "repairs" our childhood wounds by using a parenting model to rewrite our childhood experiences in a nurturing way. Although useful and necessary, the process does activate loss—and loss threatens our advancements and our sobriety. To successfully proceed, we need patience and support.

With time, however, a healthy recovering self begins to emerge: a self who can interact with our dysfunctional and frightened parts of self; a self who can begin the process of healing the childhood wounds. The focus begins to shift from the present to the past. We begin to realize how our fears experienced in present situations are related to the dysfunctional situations experienced in our past. We begin to see how our addictions and maladaptive behaviors protected us from our childhood pain and how our healing enables us to confront and resolve it. The technique I am about to describe can be used to do exactly this. It involves both a "repairing" and a "parenting" process. Because of that, I refer to it as "repairenting." The coined word seems to capture the essence of the technique.

"Repairenting" is done through the use of internal dialoguing and guided imagery. Internal dialoguing is used to alter the negative messages we heard as a child which in adulthood comprise our self-talk. If we were told as a child we were stupid, we often call ourselves stupid. If we were told as a child that we were ugly, we often refer to ourselves as being ugly.

## Exercise 7:

*Just for a moment, think of the words you would use to describe yourself. Use the space provided to write them down.*

1._____        6._____

2._____        7._____

3._____        8._____

4._____        9._____

5._____        10._____

*How many of these words are negative? How many of them are shaming and feed into your low self-esteem?*

_____

_____

_____

_____

_____

_____

_____

_____

_____

_____

_____

_____

_____

_____

_____

_____

_____

_____

_____

_____

_____

_____

Internal dialoguing helps to challenge these statements and to replace them with more nurturing ones. It can be done through journal writing, i.e. writing to your inner child and then recording an imagined response.

It can also occur through talking to yourself in the mirror or it can occur by picturing your inner child in front of you and asking him or her what is needed. The exercises and meditations in "*THE INNER CHILD WORKBOOK*" also help you begin to learn how to talk positively to yourself so that the result is nurturing instead of damaging.

Guided imagery is used as a tool to recreate the scenes from our childhood. Internal dialoguing is used in this process as well. The difference is that it is done in a more meditative way. We use our imagination or our mind's eye to retrieve these scenes from childhood. The scenes we retrieve may be real or imagined. The wounds may have come from our parent's innocent errors. They may have been the result of negligence or even intentional abuse. What is important is that, as children, we were unable to defend ourselves against these wounding life events.

For some of us, the life events may have been physical or emotional abuse. For others, the trauma may have resulted from the dysfunction in our families due to alcoholism, terminal illness, unemployment or divorce. And, for some, it may simply have been the trauma experienced from being raised at a time when parenting was not conducive to building self-esteem or the uncertainty from being raised at a time when our world was perceived as unpredictable and unsafe.

It doesn't matter. What does matter is that somewhere inside, we all have pain. Our pain is the result of dysfunctional interactions that took place when we were children. In order to heal—the pain must be revealed. In order to heal—the wounds of the inner child/ren must be repaired. It does not suffice to merely get in touch with the feelings of the wounded child. We must be prepared to constructively rework those feelings or else we will simply rewound our inner child and remain stuck in the maladaptive or addictive loop. We are closest to our inner child's pain the moment right before we act out. Until we learn how to deal with our anxiety and heal our pain, we are forever vulnerable to returning to our old maladaptive and addictive ways.

I talk of the inner children as though they are separate. In many ways they are. But the inner child is not a separate personality with its own time frame and memory. They are a part of us—they may be feeling states or ego states, but they are definitely a part of us. Even though they seem very real, they do not take over in the same way a multiple personality talks of his or her different selves.

There are times, however, when the inner child will recall a scene that we, as the adult-self, know never happened. These are symbolic scenes offered to us by our imagination so we have something concrete with which to work.

The first step in "repairenting" is to discover the characters within. How many "I's" do we have? Which "I" expresses our joy? Which "I" carries our shame? Who inside runs our daily lives, and which part of self criticizes every move we make? We do this by taking an inventory. We sit down and, in our mind's eye, we picture different feeling states. We then put a form to them.

## Exercise 8:

*Close your eyes now and picture a recent time when you were sad. How do you look when you feel sad? What made you sad? What other times in your life did you feel this kind of sadness? See yourself at that time. How old were you then? What did you look like? What did you need when you felt sad? Separate out as many parts of self as you can and begin to dialogue with each one. Notice which "I" is doing the talking!*

## DISCUSSION:

The part of you who orchestrates the show is usually your adult self. It is this part of self who will mediate between the different parts of self. In taking your inventory, you will begin to notice that almost all of your feeling states have a younger self attached to them. Very few feelings, if any, are new to us. The painful ones tend to be connected to painful memories. These memories provide the context from which we work. Our next step is to retrieve the parts of us who experienced this pain.

It is done by beginning to notice which interactions or situations in our current lives cause us discomfort. We then bring our focus to our discomfort by simply closing our eyes and assessing where in our bodies we feel tension. We determine the circumstances of this discomfort. Who said or did what that activated this discomfort? What feelings were triggered in response to this discomfort? We may discover we feel rage or fear, abandonment or shame. Once the feeling is labeled, we can ask which character within is carrying that feeling. We begin to see, sense or feel which part of us has been triggered. It is at this point that we ask, "When have I felt this way before?" Usually, by conducting this kind of internal dialogue, a memory or childhood scene will surface. It is through this process of guiding our imagery and dialoguing with the different parts of self that we can begin to rework past scenes.

It is done in the same way we might edit a film. We review the painful scene, see which characters, real or imagined, are in the scene. Once we know this, we can begin to have the characters interact. We can see who, in the scene, needs help. We then determine what he or she needs. Sometimes the intervention calls for responding to every character in the scene. Whatever the situation is, it is the adult part of self who enters into the scene. It is this part of self who intervenes and stops the destructive or wounding behavior, or meets the unmet needs.

If the adult self confronts a scene they feel ill equipped to handle, they can bring, into the mind's eye, other figures that can. They can bring in an expert such as your therapist, a minister or an adult whom you admire. What is nice about guided imagery and the use of our imagination is that we can create, in our mind's eye, whatever intervention is necessary. Research has shown that the body does not know the difference between what the mind sees and what actually occurs. If we can imagine it, we can experience it. If we can imagine healthy and responsible interactions taking place, we can negotiate and meet the needs of the characters in the scene. As the dialogue takes place, the tension and discomfort are addressed. As tension and discomfort are addressed, they dissipate and dissolve.

Sometimes, the interaction is very simple. Often inner children merely long for reassurance that they are now safe and valued. They may, at times, need to be rescued from an abusive scene. They may need assistance in getting their parents help so they can get on with being a child. The important thing is that their needs are heard and a response is made.

The internal dialogue is a way to insure inner children that they are no longer alone. The adult self can see things the child was unable to see. They can do things the child was unable to do. As we acknowledge this we can replace the painful memories with nurturing ones.

It is then, through the repetition of this process, that we reclaim and reparent the children within. Reconnecting with and healing our inner child's fears and disappointments is the bridge to our spontaneity, our naturalness and to the integration of the spiritual essence of our real self.

The following statements reflect behaviors which you may exhibit in your life today. They provide an overview of how your inner children may emerge in this second stage of recovery. There are also suggestions as to possible issues that may have evolved in response to these behaviors.

# Read each item carefully.
# Check those with which you now
# —or at some point in your life—
# have experienced.

## *Exercise 9:*

Those areas to which you respond with a 'yes' and to which you relate can be clues to the origin of your blocks. Once identified, they can give you clues as to which inner children may need attention in your second stage of healing.

Infant Stage *(Birth to 18 Months)—Suggests Possible Issues with Intimacy or Fear of Abandonment*

_____1.     I am afraid of getting too close to others for fear of being left or hurt.

_____2.     I experience the world as unsafe and unfriendly.

_____3.     I would like to exercise but seem to never be able to get started.

_____4.     I have difficulty defining my views of a Higher Source.

TODDLER STAGE *(18 months—3 years)—SUGGESTS Issues of discernment or of setting boundaries*

_____1.     I start an exercise program, but seldom follow through.

_____2.     I strictly abide by the rules of the Spiritual organization to which I belong.

_____3.     I say yes, when I really want to say No.

_____4.     I spend more money than my budget permits.

3—6 Year Old Stage—*Suggests Issues of Shame and Guilt, Discomfort In and With Body*

_____1.     I feel judgmental and condemning of others when they break the "rules."

_____2.     I worry a great deal about what others think of me.

_____3.     If another's opinion differs from mine, I assume theirs is wrong.

_____4.     I consider it a waste to spend money on frivolous items.

Grade School Self *(6 To 12 Years)—Suggests Issues of Inclusion/Exclusion, Laziness, Public Speaking*

_____1.     I seem to always feel I am on the outside looking in and that I never fit in.

_____2.     I pretty much stick to myself and do not socialize as much as I would like.

_____3.     I have a great deal of fear if and when I have to speak in front of others.

_____4.     I have a difficult time beginning and completing projects. I procrastinate.

Your Inner Teen *(12 To 15)—*<u>*Suggests Issues of Self Consciousness versus Self-Confidence*</u>
_____1.    I am uncomfortable with my body—it is too fat, thin, tall, short, or different!
_____2.    I have specific Spiritual beliefs, but keep them to myself.
_____3.    I have a hard time going to new places where I am a stranger.
_____4.    I would rather avoid contact with some people than deal with the discomfort I feel at being different than them.


Your Inner Adolescent *(15 To 17)—*<u>*Suggests Issues of Rebellion/Passivity and Need For Individuality*</u>
_____1.    I am afraid to speak my mind at work. I fear disapproval.
_____2.    I would love to follow my dreams but have fears about doing so.
_____3.    My spiritual values seem different and when expressed, tend to stand out.
_____4.    I fear losing a friendship or intimate relationship if I am honest.


Young Inner Adult *(17 To 21)—*<u>*Suggests Issues of Maturation, Taking Knowledge and Gifts into World*</u>
_____1.    My spiritual beliefs are not very well integrated into my daily practices.
_____2.    I have a hard time tolerating differences in my intimate relationships.
_____3.    If someone challenges my belief system, I begin to doubt its validity.
_____4.    I feel I have been unable to discover my life work.

*Take a moment now to reflect on your responses. Which ages held the most response for you? What does that information tell you about the issues that correspond to that stage of development? Now, briefly record your thoughts and feelings about these findings.*

_____

_____

_____

_____

_____

_____

_____

_____

_____

_____

_____

_____

_____

_____

_____

_____

_____

_____

_____

_____

_____

_____

_____

_____

*End Of Chapter Four*

# CHAPTER FIVE:

## RECOVERY STAGE THREE

▼

# "THE PURSUIT OF OUR SPIRITUALITY"

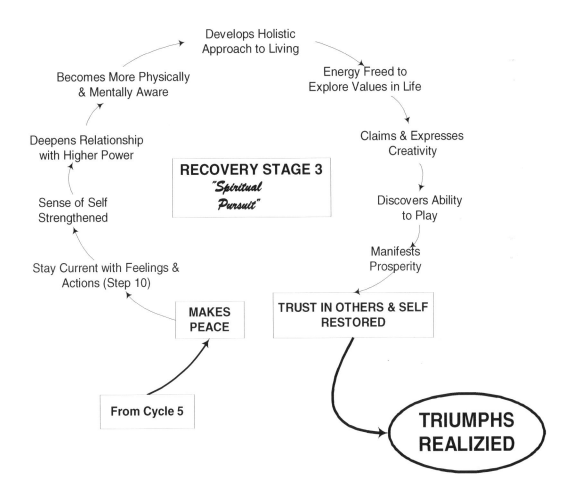

In this stage of recovery, our spiritual pursuit, we begin to search for ways to live our life more meaningfully. We begin to examine our value system. It is common to discover that many of our values are the values of others.

### Exercise 10:

*Take a moment to think about that which you most value in your own life. In other words, what is your own personal ethic—the rule by which you live? What is the origin of that ethic? How does it differ from or recreate that which was important in your family of origin? Is it an ethic that works for you in your adult life?*

_____

_____

_____

_____

_____

_____

_____

_____

_____

_____

_____

_____

_____

_____

_____

_____

_____

_____

_____

_____

_____

_____

_____

## DISCUSSION:

Since we were unable to believe in our selves, we had to look outside of ourselves for the guidelines regarding what would give our lives meaning. Although it never worked, and often left us feeling empty, we pursued this course nonetheless. Now, in this stage of our healing, we begin to redefine our values for ourselves which, in turn, enables us to then integrate new behaviors into our lives. To do this, we must sort out the difference between what we honestly value and which values we have adopted because it was adaptive and popular to do so.

Very often we discover that what we really find valuable is quite different than what we thought or were told was valuable. This exploration reveals to us our all-or-nothing thinking that developed in response to the dysfunction in our family.

## Exercise 11:

*The following is a list of opposites with which you may want to work. Choose one set and write in the space provided a few notes about the different stances each of these parts within you take.*

INNER CHILD—INNER ADULT
MASCULINE SELF—FEMININE SELF
REBEL—TYRANT
HUMAN SELF—HIGHER SELF
VICTIM—PERSECUTOR
(THINK OF YOUR OWN OPPOSITES)

_____
_____
_____
_____
_____
_____
_____
_____
_____
_____
_____
_____
_____
_____
_____
_____
_____
_____
_____
_____
_____
_____

## Exercise 12:

*Now to deepen this process, review the following list and rate the importance of each activity. Then, in the space provided, create a pie-shaped circle with slices that represents the approximate percentage of time you spend on each activity. How does the importance of each activity match with the time you spend on that activity?*

*Non-Productive Time____*        *Friends____*        *Work____*
*Primary Relationship____*        *Money____*        *Self____*
*Spiritual Endeavors____*        *Practical Tasks____*        *Family____*

## DISCUSSION:

In order to discover our values, and define our values, we need to acknowledge and neutralize our polarizations. We, again, do this by using guided imagery and internal dialogue. In our mind's eye, we separate from the polarized parts of self. We then access the Higher part of self or our 'God Within' to assist. It is this compassionate part of self who can love both the positive and negative parts of us. It is our 'God Within' and our connection to a power greater than ourselves that can balance and value the masculine and feminine parts of self, the humanistic and materialistic parts of self, and the good and bad parts of self.

Through our guided imageries and our meditations we begin to come into the middle of our polarizations. We begin to accept that there is no good or bad; there is no right or wrong. There are only choices, and these choices have lessons. All of our maladaptive behaviors and destructive coping mechanisms served a purpose. Even if there were consequences, they helped us survive.
Coming into the middle is making peace with our past. It is making peace with our addictive behaviors. It is looking at our addictions—once they have been arrested—as a gift from our soul. It is finding a balance within ourselves that permits us to look beyond the ordinary—to look at addictions and the underlying fear, shame, abandonment and rage from an angle which can propel us to the next level of our growth.

The following chapters of this book invite you to look at things from a new perspective and then concludes with offering you a step by step process you can work with your grief and dissolve your shame, guilt and fear. You will be invited to "look down the rabbit hole" and decide for yourself how far you want to go.


*End Of Chapter Five*

# CHAPTER SIX:

## AN OVERVIEW

▼

# "THE BEGINNING;
# MIDDLE AND UNKNOWN"

---

### TRAUMATIC EVENT LEADS TO ESSENTIAL WOUND
Psyche experiences trauma—basic assumption about world is shattered
↓

### EXPERIENCES SHOCK
Goes numb in response to the fear we cannot cope and will not survive
↓

### DEVELOP POST TRAUMATIC
### STRESS DISORDER (PSTD)
Develops pattern of knee-jerk emotional responses linked to this trauma
↓

### EMOTIONS CIRCULATE THROUGH BODY—NEUROPEPTIDES BOMBARD RECEPTORS
### WITH NEGATIVE VIBRATION
Every cell in body becomes conditioned to expect,
repeat and, ultimately *crave* this experience—i.e. becomes addicted to it
↓

### ENTERS INTO OUR
### CO-DEPENDENT BARGAIN
Unconscious agreement made with parent who could make us safe,
but didn't—aimed at controlling and managing our terror
↓

### DNA BECOMES CODED WITH *FUNCTIONAL* SHAME
Pattern in DNA develops a twist and slight bend—
DNA blueprint repeatedly carries shame-based code
↓

### PATTERN BECOMES THE STORY OF OUR LIFE—THE DRIVING FORCE OF OUR
### CHERISHED SABOTEUR AND OUR ADDICTIVE BEHAVIOR UNTIL WE INTERVENE AND
### GRIEVE THE ORIGINAL WOUND, ALTER THE DNA AND NEUTRALIZE THE
### DISTURBANCE IN OUR BODY'S CHEMISTRY.

Each of us has that climatic moment in our lives when we realized we were not safe. The circumstances may vary but the impact was the same—we became frozen. That moment in time is referred to as the **essential wound**. In response to our essential wound we **go into shock.** This blocks our feelings of loss and abandonment but ultimately emerges as terror, rage, shame, fear or any other intense emotion. This intensity of feeling evolves into symptoms related to **Post Traumatic Stress Disorder.**

The intense emotions circulate through the body bombarding our cells with the panic and fear of loss. When the reality of our loss erupts—the emotions are so great that the only way we can manage them is by trying to change, control or fix something. We begin to believe that what went wrong was our fault, that we are in some way deficient. We do not have the tenacity, at such a young age, to understand the problem might be with our parents or our environment—that consideration would leave us too vulnerable. Instead, it is more comfortable to assume the problem is with us.

We enter into what I call the co-dependent bargain. We make an unconscious agreement with the person we deem could protect us if only we were good enough, perfect enough, quiet enough to warrant them to love us enough to want to keep safe. We make feeble attempts to be better but, because we do not know what we did wrong, our attempts fail. We experience shame for not being good enough—we assume if we can just figure out how to be good enough then maybe we will be deserve to be protected and kept safe.

These frantic attempts are aimed at warding off the anxiety and terror of feeling unsafe. This anxiety creates stress. Our bodies' become use to the electrical impulse of the stress. Our DNA becomes coded with a shame-based response and we begin to attract that which we most fear. With time we come to expect it—crave it—create it. Anytime we are exposed to a situation which even remotely resembles our essential wound we experience the same trauma. Our cherished saboteur protects us and defends us in the same old addictive manner. The cycle continues until we intervene; grieve the original loss and re-program the codes of our twisted DNA.

> **It is a scientifically-proven fact**
> **that our mind does not know the difference between**
> **what is real**
> **and what is imagined.**
> **What we conceive we achieve.**

*"What the Bleep Do We Know?"* is taking the metaphysical and recovery worlds by storm. The movie's storyline weaves a woman's addictive battles with quirky animation to depict the impact our thoughts have on every cell of our body. Sprinkled between the real and imaginary scenes are interviews with some of the world's most renowned quantum physicists, spiritualists and alternative healers who substantiate the movie's suggestions with compelling research and extraordinary possibilities.

One significant scene features the work of Dr. Masaru Emoto who *"...discovered that crystals formed in frozen water reveal changes when specific, concentrated thoughts are directed toward them. He found that water from clear springs and water that has been exposed to loving words shows brilliant, complex, and colorful snowflake patterns. In contrast, polluted water, or water exposed to negative thoughts, forms incomplete, asymmetrical patterns with dull colors."*

> *When you focus positive, loving thoughts on your dreams*
> *your mind starts the process of creating them—*
> *UNLESS*
> *those thoughts get ambushed by your doubts and fears*
> *which then create chaos and frustration.*

If terror, betrayal, fear of abandonment or shame are attached to the manifestation of our dreams, those dreams will eventually be annihilated with negativity. If our dreams are based on the values of others instead of our own internal values and desires—we deny the essence of our true self. The manifestation of our dreams is contingent on our being connected to our true self. When we are not connected, we feel a loss—not only of our dreams—but also a loss of our true self!

This loss of our true self evolves from our adapting to become who we think we need to be in hopes of feeling accepted and loved. Loss activates the process of grief. It is involuntary. It is a natural, predictable series of emotional responses we engage in any time we experience loss of any kind. These emotional responses affect the way we think and the manner in which we express our emotions.

*"What the Bleep Do We Know?"* offers its audience the latest scientific research supporting the existence of a bio-chemical component linked to these emotional responses. What you think, feel and say plays such a profound role that you literally can (and unconsciously do) use your thoughts, feelings and statements to impact your cells.

Athletes know this. Cancer-survivors know this. They have long known the power of positive, deliberate intention and affirmation. They employ these techniques with great success.

What most of us do not keep in mind, on a day-to-day basis, however, is the fact that when our thoughts, feelings and statements are negative—they produce negative results. Our cells flat-line…become lethargic…and are programmed to energetically attract exactly what we intend. If we tell ourselves we are fat, our cells create fat. If we tell ourselves we are a failure, we creative situations in which we fail. If we fear getting hurt, we attract hurtful situations. This pattern of negative belief systems, self-negating feelings and incriminating self-talk begins in childhood in response to the first moment we are confronted with not feeling safe.

### "The Beginning"—The Essential Wound

Each of us experienced that climatic moment when we realized we were not safe. It is part of the human experience. Hal Bennett, in his book entitled ***Follow Your Bliss*** was the first to refer to this moment as the **essential wound**. Our psyche experiences a trauma which shatters our basic assumption about our world. This trauma can be a result of neglect, sexual or physical abuse or mental cruelty through shame and belittlement. It can be experienced in this lifetime or can even be carried over from a previous lifetime. The DNA blueprint of our first remembered soul experience of being unsafe is carried in the etheric body and impacts the force field of our current incarnation.

In response to this realization, irrespective of its origin, our psyche goes into shock. We either dissociate from the emotion of the event or bury recall of the event, thus banishing the memory deep into the unconscious mind. The stress of these traumas, however, gets recorded in the electrical systems of our bodies and ultimately emerges as symptoms of what is called **Post Traumatic Stress Disorder.**

### Post Traumatic Stress Disorder-PTSD

Until recently it was thought PTSD affected only combat veterans. Now scientists know that, in fact, not only are survivors of atrocities such as the Holocaust, torture, war, natural disasters, catastrophic illnesses, and horrific accidents susceptible to **PTSD**—but anyone who is exposed to an on-going threat to his or her safety, such as physical or sexual abuse, rape, domestic violence, family alcoholism, or any experience which threatens one's basic survival can develop a form of **PTSD**. Remarkably, this holds true even if a person witnesses a traumatic event. If, as a child, you observed the abuse of your mother or the abuse of a sibling—you can develop debilitating symptoms from just having been a witness.

Traumas of such great magnitude shatter our basic assumption about the world and our personal safety. The impact can leave us feeling alienated, distrustful or overly clinging. These responses are buried and surface only when there is a trigger which brings these feelings back to the surface. However, underneath the surface, the electrically-charged emotions related to these traumas are forever coded in our bodies and are conditioning our cells to attract exactly that which we most fear. The process becomes circular—our fear perpetuates this **Post Traumatic Stress** response and our **PTS** response perpetuates our fear. This fear creates anxiety. Anxiety is the first stage of grief. We are perpetually responding to the never-ending loss of our true self. Why? Because when we feel unsafe, we deny our true self and develop the adapted self as we become who we think we need to be in order to be loved and protected.

## The Bio-chemical Perspective

Dr. Candace Pert, a neuroscientist who is also featured in the film *"What the Bleep Do We Know?,"* provides a very compelling bio-chemical explanation for the circular impact of our perpetual grief. When asked why we keep getting into the same kinds of relationships, having the same kinds of arguments, repeating the same patterns she replies,

*"…Every emotion circulates through our body as chemicals called neuropeptides—"short-chain" amino acids—that talk to every cell of our body deciding what is worth paying attention to.*

*When these peptides repeatedly bombard the receptor sites, the sites become less sensitive and require more peptides to be stimulated. Receptors actually begin to crave the neuropeptides they are designed to receive. In this sense our bodies become addicted to emotional states. When we have repeated experiences that generate the same emotional response, our bodies develop an appetite for these experiences. Like addicts, we will draw experiences toward us that give us that fix…"*

> *If we are constantly being exposed to neglect and abuse, we start paying attention. We develop an almost hyper-vigilant anticipation of the abuse—and when we anticipate it we attract and create it.*

Lynn Grabhorn, in her best-selling book entitled <u>Excuse Me, Your Life Is Waiting</u>, states that *"Modern-day physicists have finally come to agree that energy and matter are one and the same…everything vibrates, because everything—what you can see and not see—is energy. Pure, pulsing ever-flowing energy. Just like the sound that pours out of a musical instrument, some energy vibrates fast from high frequencies and some vibrate slow from low frequencies…The energy that flows out from us comes from our highly-charged emotions which create highly charged electro-magnetic wave patterns of energy, making us powerful—but volatile—walking magnets. Like attracts like. When we're experiencing anything that isn't joy or love, such as fear, worry, guilt…those emotions are sending out low-frequency vibrations…they're going to attract only cruddy stuff back to us…. It is always a vibrational match."*

In my 30 years of experience in helping individuals arrest their addictive behavior and heal their childhood and Soul wounds, I have observed this same dynamic from a slightly different angle. I have observed that most of us, when conditioned to anticipate a certain response, attempt to manage the anxiety and fear which accompany that anticipation. Our psyches cannot sustain the on-going experience of anxiety which develops into the symptoms of our PTSD. In an attempt to manage our emotions we flip between the second, third and fourth stages of grief which are bargaining, rage and despair.

### "The Middle"—Co-dependent Bargain Versus Self-preserving Rage And Despair

When individuals muster up enough courage to begin the process of confronting their childhood pain, it soon becomes apparent that at a very young age—when faced with an experience which shattered their basic sense of safety—they either became very active in early co-dependent behavior; lashed out in anger at others; or shut down, became sullen, depressed and closed off to feeling anything. I call this the *fight, flight or make it right* response! All responses are attempts to cover up the underlying feeling of loss related to believing we are not good enough to be loved and protected. We begin to believe the problem is with us. Our parents are not protecting us or making us feel safe because there is something wrong with us. This is the source of all of our negative self-talk and it sets off the cycle of the blame/shame game.

### The Cycles Of Blame And Shame

Our shame is the source of our self-incriminations. We assume we need to be perfect in order to be loved and when we fail, we feel shame or we project the feelings out onto others and blame them for our deficiencies and disappointments. We super-impose the experiences of our past onto the situations of our present. The faces of strangers become the faces of those who betrayed and disappointed us. We forever get caught in the cycle of feeling shame for not being good enough or placing blame on those who disappointed and hurt us. The blame/shame game creates a cycle which is never-ending…and that cycle is the process of grief. The process of grief has five stages. The first is panic and is experienced in the form of our PTSD. To manage this panic we fluctuate between the second, third and fourth stages of grief.

If we get caught in the loop of the second stage, we bargain with the experience by attempting to make deals with the lost object in hopes of retrieve it. If our loss is a sense of safety, we try to retrieve that safety by fixing the situation which resulted in the loss in the first place. If a loss such as this occurs in childhood, we develop the behaviors which try to win back the favor of the disapproving or abusive parent. Our bargain goes something like this…*Mommy, if I am a good little girl and never make you angry—then will you love me enough to make me feel safe.* Of course, we can never be perfect enough to be reinstated this sense of safety. But we can forever be caught in the bargaining stage of grief enacted through our co-dependent behavior of trying. We can spend lifetimes trying!

When this does not work, we can shift between the third stage and fourth stages of grief—anger and despair. If the anger is turned outward and projected onto others, you are operating in the third stage of grief. If the anger is turned inward in the form of depression or despair, you are operating in the fourth stage of grief. Until our grief is processed through expression and release, we are forever caught in the vicious cycle. Our PTSD activates our need to manage this discomfort. We react by either a fight (anger), flight (despair) or make it right (co-dependency) response. We may find moments of peace—but the cycle of our grief is raging just below the surface and emerges whenever we encounter a situation which resonates with our original, essential wound.

**The Shame Of Our Imperfections**—The motivating force behind the grief process—and its perpetual re-enactment—is our feeble attempt to ward off the insurmountable fear of abandonment and loss resulting from the shame of our imperfections. The panic which accompanies this ever-present fear is intolerable. It is this panic which continually circulates through our body sending messages to our cells that ***not only are we not safe (which triggers panic) but our lack of safety is our fault (which triggers shame).*** We come to believe that we are not worthy and lovable enough to be protected. We unconsciously hold onto the hope that if we can just be good enough—perfect enough—"they" will come through for us and be able and willing to love us and make us feel safe. This inner belief becomes the foundation of our need to be perfect. Our pursuit of perfection gives us a focus for the tension created by the fear that we may fail.

But we do fail. We fail because there is no such thing as perfection. And when we fail, we end back in the middle of the tumultuous emotions of our essential wound—the fear—the panic—the disconnection from our true self. We end up back in the cycle of grief.

This cycle is the essence of the twists and bends in our DNA make–up. It is the root of our energy disturbances and energetic imbalances. It is this bio-chemical response which reinforces this pattern over and over and keeps continually bombarding the receptor sites with the peptides which disarm us.

### "The Unknown"—Let The Healing Begin

In order to become fulfilled and healthy adults we have to intervene in this cycle. We have to revise our *false belief* that we are not good enough and challenge our *pursuit of perfection*. We have to grieve the original loss of safety—express and process the anger and despair of the **Post Traumatic Stress** associated with our loss; and ultimately reprogram the cellular coding of our DNA.

**Revising Your False Belief—Challenging Your Pursuit Of Perfection**—This process deals with the mental body and the belief systems which developed in response to our not feeling safe. The mental body or mind carries the need to understand. It is the part of us who reads with such diligence to try to make sense of what happened and what needs to happen for things to change. Knowledge is power. When we come to know that the only true source of safety is the divine, we step into our empowerment and can orchestrate our own healing. As John Bradshaw stated in the mid-eighties, "There is no human security!"

The only way to challenge the belief system of our perfectionism—the source of our shame—the belief that we are not good enough—is to operate from the illuminated, adult self. It is he or she who is connected enough with our Higher Source to be able to respond to and retrieve the wounded inner child or soul part who felt the loss in the first place. That wounded self will let go of the old belief system when he or she experiences a different reality in the interaction with this illuminated you. You create your own reality and therefore you are empowered to envision a new experience for this wounded self. In your mind's eye you retrieve this wounded self and create whatever reality he or she needs in order to feel safe. Remember, *the mind does not know the difference between what is real or imagined. What we can conceive we can achieve.*

**Grieving The Original Loss**—This process responds to your emotional body. It involves allowing yourself to surrender to the feelings of loss by being able to cope with the anxiety of that loss without the fear of demise. You do not cease to exist when you feel abandoned. You survived. Your adult self is proof of this. You now have a part of you who can escort the wounded self through all of the feelings of grief. You surrender to the panic and move into the franticness of trying to control the situation. You sit through this frantic need to bargain and move into the rage of the loss in the first place. You scream, shout, beat on pillows until you get the anger out of your body. Only when you have expressed your rage can you collapse into your despair. True despair is standing in the center of the void of your loss with the ability to tolerate the emptiness. You don't distract with your addictions. You don't deny with your disruptions. You stand naked in the truth of the loss and embrace its rawness without fear. Soon the tumultuous emotions of your essential wound, expressed through your PTSD, subside. They have found release and give way to a calm which can only be experienced once the truth has been spoken. This is true whether you are dealing the memory of an inner child or the recall of an aspect of your Soul. When the emotions have been released, the circuitry of both the physical and etheric bodies is forever changed and you are in a position to download a new program into the DNA make-up of each cell.

**Reprogramming Your DNA**—DNA is a large molecule, shaped like a double helix and found primarily in the chromosomes of the cell nucleus. The DNA contains the genetic information of the cell. The DNA forms a double helix, two elongated molecular chains (like staircases) that wrap around each other. DNA tells our cells what they have been, what they will continue to be, and what they will become. The DNA is the blueprint for our life processes. Each cell of our bodies contains the complete genetic code for the whole body.

According to Margaret Ruby, founder of *The Possibilities DNA Vibrational Healing School* "*...Our bodies communication systems have been broken down due to feelings from limiting beliefs. There is a vibrational interference pattern attached to this limiting belief, causing negative, low vibrational emotions, which affect and distort our DNA...When two energy waves (thoughts and feelings) pass the same point and are out of phase, they interact and create a low vibrational, low wave interference that can, in turn, create physical or emotional imbalance...DNA then replicates with this interference pattern which has a twist and slight bend to it...*

Dr. Joe Dispensa also featured in the film "What the Bleep Do We Know?" comments that "*...the remarkable component to this dynamic is the fact that as our cells split—and they do split and recreate—they carry the energy of the old cell. It does not split with a fresh start. A cell's off-spring carries the imprint of the parent cell at the time of the split. Negativity begets negativity and positive reinforcement begets positive reinforcement!*"

There are trillions of cells in your body; within each and every cell is the nucleus, the mastermind, for the blueprint of your life. If this blueprint is faulty—the communication between each cell is faulty. By activating your DNA and accessing the vibration of purity found in the adamantine particle located in your heart, you connect yourself once again with your senses and intuition and can neutralize the interference patterns of the DNA.

The stories recorded in your DNA determine the course of your relationships, your health and your wealth. What happens to you on your life journey is a result of what is written in the life code of your DNA. This aspect provides the multi-dimensional link for processing your grief. Once the emotions of your **PSTD**, held in the psyche through your emotional responses to your loss, have been released through the process of **embracing your grief** and **neutralized** using the vibration of the adamantine particles of pure love you **can forever change the DNA** messages of your cells and begin to **attract that which you desire.**

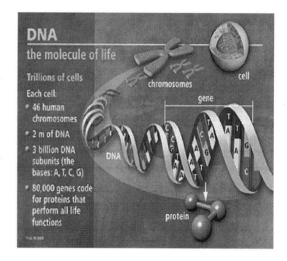

### SO WHAT THE BLEEP IS THE POINT??

The point is this—when you look at your essential wound and the cycle of your grief from the perspective of your Soul, you come to realize this whole drama has been an expression of what your Soul signed you up for this time around. It is as if this drama is the class your Soul enrolled you in this school term called life. The beauty of this healing is that it empowers us to come full circle. For the essence of our essential wound holds the thread of our Soul's lesson—and our Soul's lesson gives us the opportunity to realize the true essential wound is the moment we left the connection with our true Source in the first place. The true sense of loss—which gets projected onto our parents and loved ones—is really an expression of the loss we feel when we turn away from our Source…and so forth…and so forth.

There is no yesterday or today or even tomorrow. There is only now…this moment…this expression of Source through you. That is the true rabbit hole. Are you up for the game? Can you see the drama of your life as the entertainment center of your mind and have the courage to return to your true sense of safety found only in the Divine. Do you have the courage to embrace your grief, befriend your shame and dissolve your need to be disconnected from your Source?

*End Of Chapter Six*

## WEBSITE RESOURCES FOR THIS CHAPTER

Dr. Masaru Emoto—http://www.masaru-emoto.net/

Dr. Candace Pert—http://www.candacepert.com/

Hal Bennett—http://www.halzinabennett.com/

Lynn Grabhorn—http://www.lynngrabhorn.net/

Margaret Ruby—http://www.possibilitiesdna.com/home.html

Dr. Joe Dispersa—http://www.drjoedispenza.com/

What The Bleep Do We Know? http://www.whatthebleep.com/

Post Traumatic Stress Disorder—http://www.headinjury.com/faqptsd.htm

DNA Graphic—http://www.ucsc.edu/currents/00-01/07-03/haussler.html

Adamantine Particles—http://www.awakening-healing.com/AdamantineParticles.htm

# CHAPTER SEVEN

▼

# "GRIEF: The Antidote for Confusion and Fear"

The previous chapter invited you to look at your addictive cycle from a new perspective—but no matter how you look at it the bottom line is that in order to heal you have to feel. We do not have to belabor our grief but we do need to "process" it. The following material will hopefully assist you in befriending this life-giving process and in beginning to see it as a way to deal, moment to moment, with your past hurts, present fears and even future unknowns.

## BEFRIENDING THE PROCESS OF GRIEF— THE ANTIDOTE FOR STRESS

In order to obtain and maintain emotional health we need to be: a) connected to a Higher Source, b) responsive to the needs of our bodies and c) able to establish and maintain a nurturing support system.

Most, however, are too consumed with the stresses of every day life to have the energy needed to obtain, let alone sustain, any of the above.

If we are constantly worried about survival we do not have time to pray and meditate so we can experience a connection to God/Source. If we are constantly worried about day to day issues we do not have energy to be concerned about what we put into our bodies—we do not take the time to exercise. If we are always wrapped up in warding off the next crisis we have little time to participate in relationships in the healthy manner required to build a nurturing support system.

Few know how to manage day to day stress because few have mastered the fourth, yet chief, ingredient of emotional well being which is knowing how to embrace the process called grief.

Most of us will allow ourselves the luxury of grieving a major loss such as the death of a loved one, a divorce or the loss of a job or our home. But grief is a process with which we are involved every minute of our day. We are constantly reacting to one or more of the five stages of grief—even when we do not identify our reactions as such. The first four stages of grief are: 1) panic and denial; 2) bargaining or an attempt to control; 3) anger and 4) despair. The fifth stage of grief is surrender and acceptance.. It is experienced as a state of serenity and joy. In the moments we do not feel serenity and joy we feel stress. It may emerge as a pure sense of anxiety and panic or a need to control. It may get expressed as anger, despair or frustration. But every feeling experienced by mankind that is not serene and peaceful is a feeling that can be related to one of the first four stages of grief.

Seldom do we recognize this fact however. As has been pointed out, we instead react unconsciously to our day to day stress and do not name the feelings associated with these reactions. We cannot resolve that which are unable to name. This creates even more anxiety and panic. Many of us are perpetually caught in a state of panic masked by confusion. When this state becomes unmanageable we numb out with compulsive and addictive behaviors. Consequently, stresses related to daily living never reach resolution. They just continue to accumulate until we reach a breaking point and erupt with emotion or numb ourselves into complete oblivion with our addictions.

So what is the solution? In this day and age is it possible to live life peacefully, non-addictively—with joy and promise? What is it that we most fear? Is it alienation? Childhood wounds? Adult fears of survival?

All of these carry their own weight but *the underlying cause for engaging in compulsive and addictive behaviors is the simple fear that we will not be able to cope.*

Whether it is in the area of career, family, prosperity, love or creativity—we fear that what we have may be taken away and what we want may never manifest. The underlying fear that we will be unable to cope with the loss of dreams, hopes, friends, money, jobs, or material possessions unconsciously weighs on us as we are bombarded constantly by the inevitability of such crises. How do we ward off the anxiety of our fears, doubts or resentments? What is the process that can bridge us from seeing the world from the eyes of our human self—our every day adult self who experiences trial and suffering—to viewing the world through the eyes of our Higher Self who can observe the world and its events as opportunities for expansion? It is the process of grief.

*Embracing the process of grief is the antidote for our fear*
*that we will be unable to cope.*

Most, however, relate to grief as a process which is endured and revered only when there is a major loss—a measurable loss that has a beginning and an end. Grief is actually a natural response we have to the very challenges we each face on a daily basis. But if our grief is not processed and embraced those challenges accumulate, erode our hope, lead to rage and despair and can even manifest as physical ailments or suicidal ideation.

If we can learn how to grieve even the most minute losses like the momentary loss of self esteem or the loss we feel when a friend does not meet up to our expectations we can successfully deal with our moment to moment feelings and return to a state of serenity. Serenity? Serenity is not a state of mind that becomes fixed. It is a state of mind we continuously attain, lose and regain. But how? Through the process of grief.

By being able to deal with and resolve the anxiety which accompanies our daily losses and embrace the momentary anger and disillusionment, we are able to return to a state of resolution and trust. When we feel trust we can stay connected to our source. We can nestle safely in the comfort of the arms of our Higher Power and feel bigger than our fears. Most of us are constantly caught in a battle with our fears and our fears keep us distracted from trusting. We are either in the process of being afraid or in the process of trusting and feeling grace. We cannot be in both places at the same time.

What can we do when we slip from the safety and comfort of trusting our Higher Power into the depths of fear that we will not survive? We can embrace the process of grief.

We are actually already involved in the process of grief on a daily basis. We just do not identify it as such. For instance, one experiences the five stages of grief when confronting the simple loss that accompanies missing a phone call. Picture for a moment those times you have come in to your house with your arms full of groceries. The phone is ringing. Your hurriedly drop the bags and rush to the phone. In these days you may check Caller ID and identify that the caller is definitely someone with whom you want to speak, but just as you do this your voice mail kicks on and you have missed the opportunity to receive that long-awaited call.

What is your response?

Whether identified as such or not, it is most often the first stage of grief. Denial. You may find yourself clicking the receiver as if you can "will" the person back. Then you slip into the second stage of grief bargaining with the dead phone as you hear yourself plea, "Please don't hang up," even though the other party has already done so. This is often followed by an expression of anger or disappointment. "Damn, why did you hang up? Why could I have not gotten there sooner?" For some the response may be even more colorful! This reaction is quickly absorbed into a despair or sadness that the opportunity has been lost. What happens then? The sadness gives way to the knowledge that the person will indeed call back. Or you recall that you have that *69 on your new phone package and you instantly try to reach the caller.

However you come to terms with this incident, resolution does ensue. You have denied the phone call was missed; tried to plea for that fact to be different; felt anger in response to the loss which then gave way to despair followed simply by the resolution that you can either reach them or they will call you back. In a period of about 10 seconds you have experienced the process of grief.

If you want to be equipped with the tools to live your life non-addictively with feeling, then embrace the process of grief. Befriend this process. Use it as a way to work through all of life's challenges and disappointments. Don't deny them—but resolve them by identifying the stages of grief that you experience in response to your daily losses. Humbly move through those stages so you can return to a state of grace and resolution.

If you do not process these feelings they can manifest emotionally in your co-dependent behavior and keep you stuck in the bargaining stage of grief. You can get locked into the third stage of grief which is anger by becoming edgy or critical, or in the stage of despair which is masked by lethargy and depression—then emerges somatically in illnesses or physical ailments. But if you are willing to actively engage in the process of grief you will have a method by which you can deal with whatever life hands you.

Learn how to breathe through your anxiety, let go and give up your attempts to control the outcome of situations over which you have no control. Give yourself permission to beat on a pillow, scream in the mirror or throw a tantrum in the safety of your own home as you rid yourself of the energy of your anger. Learn how to befriend the void and emptiness of your despair so that place within you can be cleansed and prepared for you to bring in something new. Find that point of reference within for your serenity and then make that your goal to constantly process whatever keeps you from sustaining that vibration of calm and connection.

Part of the human experience is to bump up against glitches in your day to day life. **No matter how good you are**—you are going to have to deal with life's challenges. You are going to get stuck in traffic jams. You are going to get hooked into old family roles or simply have "bad days." But if you can become comfortable with the process of grief you can live fearlessly, with the assurance that you will indeed be able to cope. And if you can cope, you can love. If you can cope you can succeed!

# A GENERAL OVERVIEW OF THE FIVE STAGES OF GRIEF

Our common point of reference for the need to grieve is the loss of a loved one, of our home by disaster or debt, of our health through illness or accident, of our job or a relationship—of our physical expertise, or even our life style through a move or any change in our home life, marriage, parenthood etc. But loss occurs anytime we experience a feeling of not being safe. We lose a sense of our self-esteem through shame, neglect, abandonment or abuse.

## OUR ORIGINAL LOSS—The Essential Wound

Again, our **essential wound** occurred at the precise moment we realized we were not safe. It is at this time we went into panic and experienced the terror we would not survive.

## STAGE ONE—DENIAL

Because we were unable to tolerate the panic, we went into shock and experienced a numbing denial of the truth. Our body stored this pain in its electrical circuitry and we developed a Post Traumatic Stress Disorder. Some of us dissociated—went into a dark whole—an aspect of our soul perhaps split off—went into darkness. The rest of our system went into denial. (We might experience it as a lack of affect where an emotional component is missing.) We split off because we could not endure the pain. As you have witnessed in the material presented before—we experience this loss, and the energy has to be diverted because we do not have the coping mechanisms to process the emotions. It is from this arena our addictive behaviors emerge. The energy gets acted out instead of the loss getting resolved.

## STAGE TWO—BARGAINING

The diversion of the anxiety however only works for so long. When we are not acting it out we are engaging in an attempt to control, change or fix the situation. It is our attempt to ward off the feelings of loss over which we feel we have no control. Our bargaining attempts are another way to maintain denial of the loss. They keep us engaged in the belief we can do something to alter our loss and therefore we feel a false sense of safety. Remember, the co-dependent bargain was made in childhood in response to the essential wound. We tried to bargain with the person we either felt left us or was in a position to protect us but didn't. This bargain becomes ingrained in our unconscious behavior and can get played out in every major relationship we have because, from then on, we are forever trying to recreate that situation unconsciously seeking resolution.

The co-dependent bargain thus becomes a pattern of relating which simply begets more of the same—rejection, shame, hurt and blame.

The purpose of the original contract made with a parental figure or with God was to agree to do something in exchange for being protected and kept safe. The problem was that the other party was either unaware of this agreement or unable or unwilling to live up to this agreement. Consequently, we end up feeling betrayed and rageful when we finally admit our bargain has not been kept.

As adults we weave the shame of this failure into our self–talk and it becomes the basis of our internal critic and our projected, judgmental self. The culprit who perpetuates this self-talk and protects us with maladaptive coping mechanisms is our cherished saboteur.

## STAGE THREE—A N G E R

Anger seeps in when our denial and bargaining no longer work. We become angry at the loss, agitated at the loss. The first phase of our anger is discharged through our being cranky and critical—and through our complaining. This lets off steam without our ever having to truly embrace the full essence of our anger. This allows us to keep one foot in the door and one foot out.

Ultimately we transition into speaking our truth—and because we have been mute for so long—our first expression is usually with volume. This final stage of our anger severs the hope that things will change and allows the truth of the situation to be realized and verbalized.

**ANGER IS ENERGY AND MUST BE RELEASED.** The anger you will experience in your inner work is anger experienced before you had the knowledge and tools to spiritualize it—irrespective of what lifetime you are dealing with. Because it was experienced in the physical domain and stored in our physical forms it is necessary to discharge it physically in a responsible and constructive way.

If the grief of our inner children or Soul Selves goes unexpressed it comes out in covert and maladaptive ways. The adult self then overreacts to triggers in every day life and dumps his or her anger inappropriately. This results in inner child, as well as spiritual, shame. If expressed appropriately and safely, the anger felt in response to every day life can be acknowledged and expressed in non-aggressive ways. Since **anger is truth unspoken**, the adult can assess when his or her truth is unspoken or has been spoken, but ignored and take the appropriate action without consequence. This is setting good boundaries. **Our ultimate anger is anger at our self—at our cherished saboteur or at our Soul.**

If this anger is not neutralized through expression it is my belief that it ultimately becomes our contribution to the threat of nuclear war and the destruction of the planet/universe…so again it is imperative to learn effective and responsible ways to discharge it.

## STAGE FOUR—D E S P A I R

The appropriate response to loss once the anger has been managed is sadness. This is accompanied by an emptiness which makes way for our truth to be acknowledged and contained…. we admit the loss and express the appropriate feelings of sadness. The emptiness provides the opportunity to reclaim the feelings of being able to, once and for all, to hold the emotions of the trauma or the fear of being alone so we can feel safe enough to stand in our truth.

When we can finally embrace and feel our despair our truth can be acknowledged and contained. We are able to admit our loss, stand in the void of our loss and express the appropriate feelings associated with our essential wound. This stage of grief gives our adult self the opportunity to once and for all contain, and therefore express, the emotions of the wounded self so it is safe for the lost part of us to return. It is trusting ourselves enough to stand in the center of the void of our loss and feel secure that we will survive.

This emptiness is/was most often filled with and/or avoided by our addictive behaviors. The task is to learn how to cope with this emptiness without derailing and activating our addictions.

## STAGE FIVE—SURRENDER AND ACCEPTANCE

Surrender and acceptance occur when we have been able to speak our truth and contain the anxiety of standing in the void and emptiness of what we have realized, admitted and released. If we can contain that fear and loneliness we can claim our ability to withstand the desire to fill up with something that is not for our highest and best. The space left within us—like an empty room is then cleared and purified so it can be filled with only those aspects of our life which reflect our truth. Once our despair and anger have been processed we can come into the higher understanding of this situation and stand in a place of forgiveness and acceptance. We can see this situation through the eyes of our higher self and revere the lesson that has been learned.

When, as adults, we can finally let go, we can free up the energy we have had tied up in our grief. We can bring home the wounded self and tuck him or her into the sacred parts of our hearts and know they will forever be safe. Once done, we are in a position to make our amends—to our wounded self, to our bodies, to anyone else we feel we have wounded in the process of our journey towards letting go.

## OVERVIEW OF THE STAGES OF GRIEF
## ASSOCIATED WITH ADDICTION AND RECOVERY

What is grief in response to our addictions? Grief is a response to loss. We most definitely experience loss in response to our addictions. We can lose our home by disaster or through debt that is related to our use. We can experience grief because of the loss of our health, the loss of our job; a relationship; our self-esteem through shame; our physical expertise impaired by injury or illness that is drug related.

Our addiction can even impact our lifestyle style through a geographical move or any change in home life, marriage, parenthood that is directly related to our chemical addiction or abuse. There can often be a great deal of loss associated with our chemical use or addictive habits and this loss becomes apparent when we enter into recovery. We not only grieve what we lost because of our addictions. Once in recovery, we must grieve the loss of the addiction itself.

Recovery often requires we give up friends and places which are associated with our use. It requires we give up the chief coping mechanism which has been our friend from the time we turned to our chemicals seeking relief from discomfort. Recovery can involve feeling grief over the loss of being numb—for when we enter first stage recovery we are no longer numbed by our drugs. Instead, we find ourselves flooded by feelings and a sense of anxiety which may not even make sense and with that anxiety comes the first stage of grief.

### STAGE ONE IN GRIEVING OUR ADDICTIONS: *Panic and Denial*

Our first response to loss is panic. We go into the fight or flight response. This is the foundation for our post traumatic stress disorders. We most often respond by shutting down. We go into a state of shock (also called psychic numbing). We dissociate—go into dark hole or we act out in an addictive manner. Panic and anxiety are the physiological expressions of our abandonment and fear. We fluctuate from feeling the panic and then acting it out so we can return to the state of numbness of our denial.

But it doesn't last long—it bubbles to the surface again and so we act out even more as our addictive patterns progress and become addictive diseases if our bodies cannot tolerate what we are ingesting. As our addictions progressed we lost sight of what the panic was even related to—we just simply experienced a restlessness which was quieted by our drug.

### STAGE TWO IN GRIEVING OUR ADDICTIONS: *Bargaining*

When our addictions no longer keep us numb we shift to attempting to keep our system in denial through our bargains. We make deals with the objects of our loss—we try to win them back or control their leaving—when our addictions take over we begin to make deals with our addictions—we make false promises and empty threats. Searching for ways to ward off the inevitable pangs of the loss we engage more and more in bargains and deals that never materialize but forever keep us in the stream of negotiation with self and others.

In recovery we can begin to bargain with our program…it is called stinking thinking. We begin to think we can control our use and become preoccupied with ways we can manage to control our use. If we do not talk about these thoughts we can be on the way towards relapse.

## STAGE THREE IN GRIEVING OUR ADDICTIONS: *Anger*

Our anger regarding giving up our addictions seeps in when the bargaining and denial no longer work. We become angry or agitated at our loss of control. This is often expressed as crankiness or criticalness.

Once we are in recovery we can experience our anger in the form or irritation. We can be angry because we are different than others, angry because we cannot "control" our use. Sometimes we do not even know what we are angry at…we are just angry.

The task of working with our anger in the first stage or recovery is to simply manage it so that we do not return to our addictive behavior. It is necessary to learn new coping mechanisms to accomplish this task. Some examples are: deep breathing, writing, sharing in meetings (venting), exercising, reading program material.

The resolution of our anger does not occur until we are further in recovery and have established a viable and workable program which consists of a sponsor and a commitment to meetings.

## STAGE FOUR IN GRIEVING OUR ADDICTIONS: *Despair*

The appropriate response to loss once the anger has been managed is sadness. This is accompanied by an emptiness. This emptiness was most often filled and avoided by our addictive behaviors. In recovery our task is to learn how to cope with this emptiness without using. We can do this in the same manner as we managed our anger—by breathing, talking and writing, exercising.

## STAGE FIVE IN GRIEVING OUR ADDICTIONS: *Surrender and Acceptance*

This is the stage when peace can be made. In first stage recovery we cycle in and out of this state of mind. It is assisted by learning how to turn it over and to allow God to run the parts of our lives which have become unmanageable.

Although in early recovery it is important not to delve into the issues of your childhood—it can be useful to identify, understand and therefore accept that certain feelings can be traced back to different stages in your childhood. It can normalize your experience knowing that this discomfort will be dealt with more fully once you have established a solid recovery program and have learned how to cope with your day to day feelings without relapse.

## *End Of Chapter Seven*

# CHAPTER EIGHT:

▼

# "WINNING THE GAME OF GRIEF"

The remainder of this material offers you a series of processes you can use to begin working with your own grief. As you become more familiar with these stages you naturally begin to find your own methods for befriending this process. You come to understand that embracing the difficult feelings by having the courage to breathe into them expands your capacity to experience your pleasure, passion and joy. You begin to appreciate that you are constantly on a teeter-tooter between love and fear with everything else falling somewhere in between. Life itself becomes as entertaining as a board game—where you land reflects where you need to go next.

**PROCESSES FOR PANIC AND DENIAL:**

1. MAKE A LIST OF THE WAYS YOU ACT OUT TO KEEP YOURSELF FROM FEELING THE PANIC OR DISCOMFORT OF YOUR LOSS…in other words, ways you have kept, you keep or you get yourself back into denial! This will help you begin to recognize the beginning pangs of loss.

2. TAKE A PIECE OF PAPER AND DRAW A PICTURE WHICH SYMBOLIZES YOUR ANXIETY. This gets these feelings out—gives them form.

3. DIALOGUE WITH YOUR ANXIETY—ASK WHO INSIDE HOLDS IT AND WHAT THAT PART OF YOU NEEDS FROM YOU. BREATHE THROUGH THE ANXIETY AND SEE WHERE IT LEADS YOU. This creates a relationship to your anxiety so you can respond to it instead of collapse into it.

## PROCESSES FOR BARGAINING

1. WRITE BRIEFLY ABOUT HOW YOU FEEL YOU ARE BARGAINING WITH "SHOWING UP" FOR YOUR LIFE. What might this reveal about the pain of potential losses that are inevitable as you step forth into your empowered self? What part of you benefits from your sabotaging succeeding at your goals? Who suffers and battles with a sense of failure? How does your co-dependent bargain interface in this relationship?

2. WHAT IN YOUR LIFE NO LONGER FITS AND HOW ARE YOU TRYING TO KEEP YOURSELF FROM FACING THIS FACT? Again, the co-dependent bargain is the contract we made with a parental figure or with God where we agreed to do something in exchange for feeling safe and protected. These agreements follow us into adulthood and into every relationship we have. The problem is that the other party is either unaware of this agreement or unable or unwilling to live up to this agreement so we end up feeling betrayed and full of rage when faced with the fact that our bargain was not kept. Sometimes we even extend this contract to ourselves as we make deals with our destructive or addictive behavior—convincing ourselves that we can control or manage our out-of-control behavior. This shows up in our day to day life when we bargain with our agreements and make false promises to ourselves and others which, when we do not follow through, erodes our self esteem.

3. WITH THE ABOVE IN MIND, IDENTIFY YOUR CO-DEPENDENT BARGAIN…

_____, (addressing those with whom you made/make the contract)
I WILL_____ (the sacrifice, compromise you are willing to make
IF ONLY YOU WILL _____ (what you hope to get in return)

How does your co-dependent bargain impact your day to day life? Do you see yourself living out this bargain as a way to manipulate yourself and others? How would your life change if you gave up the bargain and came into your true empowerment. What would happen if you coped successfully with your life and took responsibility for yourself by giving up the temptation to feel like a victim? Take time to really think that process through because it holds unlimited possibilities for evolvement.

4. TAKE A PIECE OF PAPER TO DRAW A PICTURE WHICH REPRESENTS YOUR ANGER. USE THIS AS A WAY TO DISCHARGE YOUR DISCOMFORT AND TO IDENTIFY YOUR PAIN. (Give it form!)

## PROCESSES FOR DISCHARGING AND DISSOLVING ANGER

1. Journal Process—respond to the following questions to explore the fabric of your anger. Once completed you will be ready to do the "weeding out" process.

> What is your unspoken truth? To whom does it need to be told? What holds you back from doing so? What do you fear will happen if you speak your truth? Are you willing to cope with those possible consequences? If not, what are you willing to cope with? How far can you go right now to speak your truth and where do you have to be mindful and protecting of yourself? Don't push if you are not yet ready to push. Forced labor seldom results in a productive birth.

2. Weeding Out Process—I originally came across this exercise in a book written in the 80's by Sondra Ray. Since then I have used this or a version of it in a multitude of ways and it never fails to weed out my saboteurs and those within me who resist change. *Instructions: Write "I am angry" in column one followed by your immediate response in column two. Continue until you can write "I am angry" in both columns with vim and vigor!! Use more paper if necessary.*

**EXAMPLE**

1. I AM ANGRY!                    1. BUT THEY DID THE BEST THEY
                                      COULD!

2.                               2.

3.                               3.

4.                               4.

5.                               5.

6.                               6.

7.                               7.

8.                               8.

9.                               9.

10. "I AM ANGRY!                 10. "I AM ANGRY!"

**What To Do About The Anger Which Will Emerge In The moment?** We have anger which is stored and anger which erupts—the following are suggestions which can be applied to both.

First surround yourself in light and ask that any anger expressed be encased in the light and sent directly to the higher source to be transformed. This will seal it so that its energy will not bleed out into other arenas.

THEN, WHEN YOU FEEL IN ALIGNMENT TO DO SO, USE ANY OF THE FOLLWING TECHNIQUES TO EXPRRESS YOUR ANGER AND TO GET IT OUT.

1. Write and/or do mirror work (deals with the mental and emotional bodies)
2. Beat on pillows—throw a tantrum, stomp—do any physical activity which gets the emotion out of the body. (emotional body)

3. Do the silent scream—screaming in a car (emotional body)

4. Exercise to make the energy manageable (note: aerobic exercise, such as jogging, etc. reduces current anger, anaerobic exercise, such as yoga, swimming etc. reaches anger that is more deeply rooted in the muscular fibers.)

5. Do an inner dialogue where you listen to your inner child's anger as the adult self. Allow it, you do not have to change it or fix it. You just have to help him or her discharge it responsibly so it does not bleed into inappropriate acting out in day to day life.

6. Make a list of critical statements you say to yourself on a regular basis—now review the list and make an affirmation you can use to negate your critical statement.

7. Make a list of your personal gripes, pet peeves, and those behaviors which irk you most when you see them exhibited in others. Then review the list—how do you see *yourself* exhibiting those same behaviors—or if you cannot relate to that angle—are they doing something you do not allow yourself to do so it mirrors a shadow side to you? If so, how do you feel about that?

## PROCESSES FOR RELEASING YOUR DESPAIR

1. Write letters to those who you feel have betrayed, neglected or wounded you. Let them know that you, as the adult, are now willing to take responsibility for the feelings of the wounded selves who have felt victimized by their actions. Forgive them so you can move on and become empowered enough to take responsibility for your younger self's fear and pain..

2. When you feel ready—write another letter to the parts within you who are ready to let go—welcome them home and make your amends and vow to them to keep them safe. Know that it is the adult self who needs to be responsible for this promise—but you can always bring in the angels or guardians to tend to your wounded self's needs. Just make sure the needs are addressed by a nurturing party.

3. Take a moment and write the truth of your loss—let your inner child—the aspect of your Soul or the wounded adult self just take a moment to:

   STATE IN BOLD PRINT HIS OR HER TRUTH WHICH NEEDS TO BE TOLD. Then, write a letter to the person to whom this truth needs to be stated.

## PROCESS OF RELEASE AND FORGIVENESS

The following ritual was given to me by a Hawaiian Elder named Josie. It is but one way to orchestrate a formal forgiveness. Please feel free to use or create your own as well.

### HAWAIIAN FORGIVENESS RITUAL—HO' OPONOPONO

FORGIVE ME_____

> If I have hurt you
>
> In any way, shape or form,
>
> In thought, word or deed,
>
> In any time, any place,
>
> Past, present or future
>
> FORGIVE ME.

AND I, _____ FORGIVE YOU

> For hurting me
>
> I any way, shape or form,
>
> In thought, word or deed,
>
> In any time, any place,
>
> Past, present or future
>
> I FORGIVE YOU!

AND MAY THE CREATOR OF ALL THINGS FORGIVE US BOTH: ALL HO'OPONOPONO

IT IS DONE…SO BE IT!

This ritual can be said between you and another, between you and your body, between you and your inner child, between your Spirit and your Personality.

It is also a common practice to ceremoniously take any notes, pictures or expressions of your grief and burn them. It cleanses and frees the emotions and symbolically transforms the energy of your pain so you can send its essence back to the Divine Light for healing. I then take the ashes of my process and go into Mother Nature to make an offering. As I do this I express my gratitude for all I have learned and re-affirm my vows to sustain the new vibration of joy I have claimed by having the courage to grieve.

*End Of Chapter Eight*

# Epilogue

*There is that moment,*
*right before*
*we engage*
*in our compulsive or addictive behaviors,*
*when we are the closest*
*to the feelings of the wounded selves*
*who feel abandonment, fear, rage, shame and despair.*
*Each time we distract*
*with our compulsions and addictions*
*we choose to ignore,*
*instead of nurture,*
*those within us*
*who so badly need our care.*
*But,*
*when we choose*
*to stay connected to our Source*
*instead of giving in to the temptations*
*of our addictions,*
*we seize,*
*at least for that moment,*
*to live our life*
*beyond our confusion and fear.*

*I honor your courage and your journey.*
*Cathryn Taylor, Independence Day, 2005*

978-0-595-36474-9
0-595-36474-8